HOW TO PRODUCTIZE YOUR SERVICES

How to Make Money while you're sleeping

Table of Contents

Section 1 – Create

Introduction

One of the reasons that many people enter the world of freelancing is for the freedom it provides them. What can be more freeing than working at home in your PJs? I know that when I began my freelance career, I thought it would be wonderful to decide when and where I would work, or even whether I wanted to work at all. It didn't take long for me to realize that this was not necessarily true. I had simply traded one boss – the one I answered to at my place of employment – for several bosses – the clients who now vied for my time.

What made matters worse is that it wasn't the fun, easy-to-deal with clients who took up my time. Instead, it was the clients who sent me multiple emails, were constantly on the phone or who requested what seemed like never-ending revisions to my work. On top of that, those were the clients who often failed to pay me on time.

Then there was the fact that I didn't feel like I actually owned the work that I did. I would use my many years of expertise to provide the client with exactly what they needed only to have the client pick it apart because they thought they knew more than I did. They would insist on things I knew wouldn't work, no matter how many times I tried to explain why the changes were not the best choice. In the end, to appease the client, I always did as they requested.

The problem with that is that I didn't feel I could put my name on the completed work. It wasn't the quality I wanted so it was useless in my portfolio. If you are a freelancer, you know this has happened to you more times than you would like.

But even those were not enough to push me into what I needed to do. The final straw was when I realized I could not increase my rates any more and, because my work was tied to my time, I could not really take on any more clients or work. I had hit the income ceiling. My income was not going to grow much more and I could probably expect to make the same thing year after year. That was when I realized a raise was not the answer. What I needed was a promotion and the only way I was going to get that promotion was to begin looking at my work as a business.

As a business owner, you are able to develop strategies that will allow you to earn income without tying that income directly to your time. Instead of focusing on the day-to-day tasks, you are able to look into the future, to plan the next thing you need to do to grow your business and to avoid spending your day jumping from one menial task to another.

Unlike a freelance career, a business is designed to grow. Instead of only growing your clientele, you can grow a team that will help you not only grow your customer base but also allow you to focus on the things that will continue to improve your bottom line. Your business becomes an asset rather than something that simply takes time. A business can be sold or you can create processes so that the business can almost run itself while you reap the benefits.

The first thing to remember when you move from freelancer to business owner is the need to productize your services. A productized service is one that gives a customer a single deliverable at a set price and scope with a value proposition, with the ability to be scaled up even without your direct involvement or time.

Isn't it time to give yourself a promotion? Over the next few chapters you will learn how to work in your business rather than on it as well as how to take a strategic approach to making changes in your business. These tips can help any type of freelancer become a business owner, whether you are a writer, designer, developer or consultant.

Chapter One – You're Getting a Promotion

It's time to get that promotion. However, you are probably asking yourself how you can possibly be promoted when you are the only one working in your company. The answer is actually very simple. Stop working in your business and begin working on your business.

As a freelancer, you spend most of your day with the nuts and bolts of your service. You may be writing code for a client's website or adding keywords to a blog post. You are in every part of the work you are doing. However, as a business owner, you must have a different mindset as to what the bigger picture is. You want to continually look for ways to make that business grow and the only way to do that is to work on the business.

For example, when you are drafting a blog or invoicing a client, you are working "in" your business. Although these things are important to your work, they are the day-to-day tasks that go into creating a finished project. Setting the marketing strategy or creating systems and procedures to make things run more smoothly are examples of working "on" your business.

The fact is that once you decide to move from freelancer to business owner, you can no longer run every aspect of the company, nor should you. Your focus needs to be on strategy and long-term goals rather than the day-to-day tasks that come with freelancing. This does not mean you can no longer be creative. You can still write blogs posts and still create graphics for the client, but you no longer need to do that on a day-to-day basis.

In addition, working on your business does not mean stepping away completely. It is possible to cut back on day-to-day management and leave the work for your team, but it is also important to keep the needs of your team in mind as well. Even if you hire the best managers or are working with the best group of sub-contractors in your business, without guidance it is easy for a company to drift away from an original concept.

For this reason, you must occasionally work "in" the business, to keep your finger on the pulse of the company, but the majority of your time should be spent working "on" the business, creating strategies and goals that will allow the company to continue to grow, even when you are not available for the day-to-day requirements.

Keep in mind that working on your business rather than in it does not mean you have to immediately go out and hire staff. In fact, it is important that you focus on hiring the right people, which may take some time. You may want to remain small and focus on growing personally. By productizing your services, you have far more control not only of what you do, but of what you don't do as well. Your business can be designed so you are freed from the tasks that detract from your creativity, either by setting things up in a more streamlined process or by creating a quality team of professionals who allow the business to grow at a slow but steady pace.

In order to accomplish this, it is important to understand how to take a strategic approach to making changes in your business.

Chapter 2 – Find Your Why

The title of this chapter may seem unusual since we are discussing a business. You know why you entered the freelance world, whether it was because you had a skill that you wanted to share, wanted the freedom to pick and choose your clientele or were simply thrust into it due to necessity. However, you also need to know why you continue to do things the way you do them and how to take steps for adjustment as necessary.

The business world is fluid, changing over time. In some industries, change is slower than molasses in January. Unfortunately, in today's rapidly changing, global business environment, industries that change slowly are decreasing at a rapid pace. Today, changes happen over months, weeks, and sometimes it seems, days. For this reason, you have to be able to change and adjust to meet those changes.

People are, by nature, creatures of habit, which makes them resistant to change, even when it is subtle. The key is to take a strategic approach to implementing change using proven factors for success.

First, take the time to learn how change will impact others, both inside and outside your organization. If you have been the sole writer of blogs for a particular client, understand that contracting that blog to someone else could have an impact on the client. More than likely, since you are just starting to move from freelancer to business owner, you won't have staff or contractors working for you. But, once you do, be sure to discuss any changes you need to make in order to minimize the impact on them as much as possible.

Be sure to consider the **emotional factors** involved in change. Too often, managers make changes based on the rational reasons for the change and ignore the emotional that are involved. Good business owners are able to take into account the emotional aspect of change in order to reduce anxiety and to promote creativity.

Changing your mindset from that of a freelancer to a business owner also requires your own set of changes. Running a business is different than working as freelancer. As a freelancer, your income is directly related to the time you put into the work. Running a business allows you to create products that don't require your direct attention, are scalable and have value even though you are not participating in a hands-on fashion. This requires you to change your own beliefs and attitudes about your business.

Change is something that you must face when you move from a freelancer to a business owner, but, when done properly, change can be very beneficial, especially if you have productized your services.

Chapter 3 – Anatomy of a Productized Service

Now that you understand the need for change in order to get that promotion you deserve, you need to understand exactly what a prioritized service is. As a freelancer, you are stretched pretty thin, trying to do multiple projects with several moving parts. A productized service is a single core deliverable with a strong return on investment. Instead of being known for the several hats you wear right now, you will be known for doing one specific thing really, really well. Clients will view your service as a necessity rather than a desire. Not only does a productized service provide benefit to the client, it also streamlines your own processes so that it produces whether you are working or not.

The best way to understand what a productized service is would be to look at the difference between products and services. Products are tangible items that a company produces that can be inspected, touched or sampled before the consumer purchases them. Scaling up a product is done by expanding the manufacturing ability or distribution of the item. A product also has ownership as the person who purchases it and the product is delivered to a customer.

A service, on the other hand, has the customer coming to the service and are often customized to suit the needs of the consumer. Services are not tangible and it is more difficult to scale up a service as they are often limited by the availability of experts in that field. You also cannot own a service and it cannot be resold to another consumer. Although the haircut you get from your stylist is yours, you cannot transfer that haircut to your sister if she likes it. You can, however, refer your sister to your stylist for the same service.

If you are a freelance writer, website designer or graphic artist, you offer your clients a service. This means that you may think the only way to build your business is to have clients come to you to get that service. By creating a productized service, you will find that your expertise can easily become a tangible product.

The key is to systematize the service so that both you and the client receive the benefits. Productizing your services establishes trust with your client and can help you become more productive. They key is to define what can be standardized in your business and what you can customize to meet customer needs. Using online tools, develop systems that automate your service process, such as a text editing and proofreading service for content.

You are probably asking "What makes a productized service so valuable?" The answer is that productized services increase profitability, increase quality, reduce risk and allow you to expand from a freelancer to a business owner much more easily.

It is important, however, to remember that not all services you offer must be productized. There may be some facets of your freelance work that you may want to keep as a separate service but it is important to keep those at a minimum and focus on building your reputation on being an expert in one particular area.

The next step in making a smooth transition from freelancer to business owner is to learn how to find your one thing. In other words, you need to know how to pick your focus so that you can successfully productize your services.

Chapter 4 – Finding Your One Thing

Freelancers often have no focus although the majority of them will insist that they do. Look back at your last year of invoices to see what you work was billed to clients. You will probably find a wide range of services that you provided without even realizing you were providing so many. A web designer may bill for everything from copywriting to site tweaks to custom coding. Although you may be good at all those things, in order for productized services to work, you need to choose one service and focus on doing that exceedingly well.

"So, how do I choose what service to focus on?" you may ask. That is actually not as difficult as you may think. Review those invoices again and determine what you made the most money doing. That is the service you need to use for your focus. For example, if you made the majority of your income writing blog posts for local real estate agencies, blog writing may be your focus. To further increase your chance of success, choose the area where you can show real results to potential clients, such as an increase in website traffic after a particular blog post.

The key to success when you choose your productized service is to make clients believe that you are willing to take over a task that they find so painful and so difficult, they are willing to pay you to do it for them. You want to position your company as the only place where a client can get exactly what they need when they need it. However, when you are choosing your focus, you also need to look toward the future to see how you can automate the entire process so that the company runs even when you aren't running it.

"There is no way my writing company can be automated," you are thinking. This is the thinking of a freelancer and not a writer. There are many online content sites available today that allow you to contract your writing needs with another writer who is just as talented and just as thorough as you are. Social media posts can be written weeks in advance and scheduled for posting when you want them to appear. There are even programs that allow you to connect all your internet-based services together (http://www.provideocoalition.com/automating-your-creative-business). No matter what type of industry you are in, there are ways to automate and streamline your services so that you can step back from the day-to-day tasks and focus more on the long-term growth of your business.

Simply, you must define what "it" is – what your Most Important Thing is – in order to focus on the one task that you can do well. Understand that the "one" task may incorporate several different tasks. For example, if you have reviewed your last year invoices and found that the majority of your income came from creating email newsletters for clients, you will need to incorporate your graphic, writing and editing skills in order to provide your clients with the best email newsletter they have ever had.

Once you have determined what it is you will focus on, you need to ask yourself several questions:

- What is the benefit to the customer?
- What will the customer get?
- How can it be automated?
- How will I brand this service?

Although you may not have the answers to all those questions yet, you will at least know what answers you are looking for.

In addition to focusing on one service to offer, another version productizing services is to offer packages, or bundles, of tasks into one service. A web designer may offer a package that includes annual maintenance, SEO and upgrades into one package. Although this seems to be contradictory to the "focus on one thing" rule, if you include similar tasks together, it actually is the same as focusing on one thing. In addition, it makes the client feel as if they are getting added value for their money.

Once you have determined what the "one thing" is that you want to offer, it is time to create a value proposition that will convince clients that you are the only company that can provide them what they need.

Chapter 5 – Your Value Proposition

Your value proposition explains to clients what you will provide for them and how you will do it better than your competition. It should describe your target market, the problem you plan to solve for that market and why you are the one that should be chosen to solve that problem. There are several steps necessary to create the perfect value proposition.

First, you must define the problem that you plan to solve. Although it may have worked in "Field of Dreams," you cannot simply build it and they will come. Instead ask yourself four questions when you are identifying the problem you want to address:

- What productized service is your company selling?
- What is the end-benefit to the client of choosing your service over another?
- Who is your target market?
- What makes your service unique and different

Once you have identified the problem, you must evaluate whether your company has a unique and valuable method for solving the problem. Your content company may offer quick-turnaround for clients that other companies do not. You may have specific expertise in web design that is not available in your area. You will need to determine what it is about your company that makes it different from others in order to convey that information in your value proposition.

When you have answered all the questions thoroughly, it is time to create the value proposition. A good value proposition should include who your target market is and what it is that is missing from the market that you can provide. You should include information about the productized service you are offering and describe exactly what problem it solves. You should also include why it is different than that offered by your competitors, whether it is a lower price, faster turnaround or expertise that others in the area do not have.

If it sounds as if a value proposition is a sales pitch, you are not far from the truth. For the value proposition to be successful, you must know your customer and you must have a clear understanding of what your productized service offers. Whenever possible, include statistics in order to get the attention of your target market. You also need to have a strong understanding of your competitors in order to address why your product is better than theirs.

Look at the value proposition from the customer perspective. Ask yourself why you would purchase your own product or service, then try to answer as if you were a customer. By placing yourself in the customer's shoes, you may see areas where your value proposition can be tweaked and adjusted so that it better meets their needs.

It is also important to understand what a value proposition is not when you are creating one. A value proposition is not a catch phrase or slogan. It is also not designed to be a positioning statement, although a positioning statement can be a subset of a value proposition.

A value proposition should be very easy to understand and communicate the results a customer will see if they choose your company. Understand that the clients may receive offers from competitors and you want the client to read your value statement and know why your company will solve the problem while the competitor may not. It should be short, able to be read in about five seconds. Avoid language that sounds like hype, superlatives and business jargon (http://www.conversionxl.com/value-proposition-examples-how-to-create/).

Try to give customers relevancy by specifically stating the problem and who you will solve it. "No time to update your social media page? We will do it for you!" This value proposition, although short, tells the customer who no longer has time to post to Facebook that you are willing and able to take that task off their hands. You can also add a specific value for your customer, such as a discount or a lower price than a competitor. Whenever possible, point out what is different between your company and another offering the same service.

Once you have created the perfect value proposition, it is time to look at pricing, something that many freelancers and start-up companies struggle with as they don't want to overprice themselves but they also do not want to work for free.

Chapter 6 – Pricing

When you sell products, it is not difficult to set the price for those products. You simply determine the percentage you want to make after the expenses of creating the product and the price is set. It is not quite as concrete when you are selling services, even those that have been productized.

Let's face it, you went into business to make a profit. Unfortunately, many small businesses fail to analyze the cost of providing services when they set their prices. As a freelancer in your PJs, you may not have considered the overhead that goes into creating your service. You still must pay your mortgage or rent, electricity, internet service and other costs in order to work at home. If your plan is to contract some of the work you have been doing, you will now have contract fees to pay that you may not have had when you were working as freelancer. These costs must be taken into account when pricing your services.

Although you may be tempted to undercut your competitors drastically in order to grab clients that is not necessarily the best solution. You want to position your company properly in the marketplace. You may want to offer slightly lower prices than your competitor, or a temporary discount, but drastically lower prices could cause a client to question whether you are qualified for the work.

Surprisingly, most small businesses do not charge enough for their services because they don't take into account the expenses that go along with providing services. Therefore, consider charging more than you think you should get for services and you may be surprised that clients do not question the cost. If a client does bulk at the cost, you have some leeway for offering a discount, making the client feel as if they are getting an even better deal from you.

Service providers have the option of charging by the hour or as a flat fee for a specific job. To determine an adequate hourly rate, add up your labor and overhead costs plus the profit you hope to earn. Divide that number by the hours you work. This is the minimum you should charge to pay your expenses, your salary and to show a profit. You can also use the annual salary you earned at your last place of employment to determine what your hourly rate should be.

Computing expenses is fairly simple. Add up any costs involved in performing your work. If you are a graphic artist, all supplies, computer programs, fees for online programs, internet service and more are expenses necessary for you to complete your work. Remember to include healthcare costs, utilities and professional memberships as well.

Determining the profit you want to make is completely up to you. Remember that salary you pay yourself is not part of the profit, it is the cost of doing business. There is really no standard profit percentage, but most business owners set their profit margin between 10 and 20 percent.

To determine billable hours, you need to know how many hours you will work and get paid for each year. If you work a 40-hour week with a two-week vacation, you will have 2,000 billable hours per year. Keep in mind that as much as 25 to 35 percent of your time will be spent on things you cannot bill until you can delegate those tasks to someone else or automate them. This includes bookkeeping and billing, marketing and long-range strategy.

One of the best tools for determining the rate you should charge is by investigating the marketplace. Talk to a professional trade association in your area or talk to others who are performing similar jobs locally. Attend trade shows or business conventions to get an idea of what the going rates are in your industry (http://www.nolo.com/legal-encyclopedia/business-services-charge-how-much-30158.html).

Some startup companies use what is known as price anchoring when they begin charging for services. In this method, the company charges a higher price and then offers a discount. This method works well when selling products to consumers, but may not be as effective in the service market. A customer may wonder what is wrong with the service if it is discounted. Therefore, offer the discount as a one-time only or signing discount, making it clear to the customer that the regular price will resume at a set date or by a certain project.

The bottom line is that pricing is about value. When you created your value proposition, you determined what it is about your company that is more valuable than the competition. Once you know what you offer that the customer finds important, it is easier to determine a price that matches the value of the service. In some ways, your price must be within market boundaries. Although you may think that the social media posts you will create are the best the client will ever see, if a local competitor is offering them at half the price, you may not get the client to even look at what you can offer them.

In some cases, however, a customer is willing to pay a higher price if they know they will get the value they need. For example, they may be willing to pay double for those social media posts if they can see an increase in traffic on their website or have people in their store mentioning what they read on Facebook. If you can show value along with your pricing, you are more likely to get a higher price than if you cannot demonstrate value to the customer.

In addition to standard pricing, there are also other common pricing strategies that are used by companies. Skim pricing is when prices are set higher than the competitor in order to create a sense that your services are better than those offered elsewhere. However, for this strategy to work, you must offer something that is not easily found elsewhere and you must deliver an extremely high-quality service.

When you use neutral pricing, you set your prices at around the same level as your competitor. This method works well if you want to offer additional services that your competitor does not. For example, if you and a competitor are offering $200 for monthly blog posts, you may offer an additional content service, such as a social media post that matches the blog topic at no additional charge. The added bonus may be enough for the client to use your service over the competitor as they feel as if they are getting something for free.

A company that uses penetration pricing offers a low initial entry price in order to draw customers from a higher-priced competitor. In most cases, the price rises over time, but many businesses have found that when the price rises, the customer leaves for a lower priced competitor. You may avoid that if you consistently provide quality services to the client regardless of the price point. A satisfied customer will be less likely to move to a competitor even when the introductory price ends.

Almost every small business owner will tell you that pricing is one of the most difficult aspects of starting a business, but by following a few tips and suggestions, you can set a price that will not only grow your business but allow you to turn a profit as well.

Once you have established your pricing, it is time to begin looking at ways to automate your business. Automation is the key to reducing your need to deal with the day-to-day tasks of your business and begin thinking more like a business owner.

Section 2 – Automate

Chapter 7 – The Path to Autopilot

Now that you have determined your focus, developed a value proposition and set your pricing, it is time to begin down the path to autopilot. As we discussed before, as a freelancer, you can grow your business by working more hours, raising your prices or cutting costs. Because a service-based freelance business is tied directly to how many hours you can work in a day, your revenue is limited. There are only so many hours in the day that you can work. Trust me, sleep is definitely not overrated. Also, keep in mind that your billable hours will be even less than the hours you have available as you need to eat, take care of your family and occasionally shower.

Let's look at raising your rates. The market will limit what you can charge for your service as we discussed previously. Once you are charging the maximum rate, it is difficult for you to increase that rate. That means, eventually, you will reach the point where you cannot make more money by increasing what clients pay you.

The final way to improve income in a freelance business is by cutting costs. Let's face it, as a freelancer, you probably have very minimal business costs already. Your internet service is a set price and the company that provides it is not likely to give you a discount simply so you can increase your revenue. You could cut the heat back in the winter and work with more clothes on or turn of the air conditioner in the summertime to save some money. None of those reductions are going to give you more time in the day to take on more work.

What this means is that you need to work smarter, not harder. The key is to add scale to your services in a variety of ways. Scale gives you more hours in the day to complete tasks and can be achieved either by adding people or increasing productivity.

As a freelancer, there is only you and the hours you have available to work. If you hire another person, you then have twice the hours available to complete tasks. The key is to hire people whose skills complement yours so that your company offers a wider range of benefits. For example, if your expertise is in the legal field, but you know nothing about the gaming industry, hiring someone with extensive gaming knowledge would add expertise to your company that you currently do not have.

The problem is that most freelancers are not in a position to hire someone immediately, even on a contracted basis. Maybe you don't have the client base yet to warrant paying someone else to do the work or you are just beginning to see your business grow and are able to keep up with client needs right now. If this is your situation, you can still scale your services by working as efficiently as possible. We have already discussed the need to productize your services to make them more easily scalable. If you have done that, you are already on the right track toward automating your processes.

There are many ways that day-to-day tasks in your business can be streamlined. Take invoicing for example. Creating, saving and sending an invoice can take between 18 and 20 different steps. Keep in mind that is just to send the invoice – it does not take into account collecting the invoice or tracking income. Consider using an automatic invoice tool such as Harvest that will automatically send your invoices for you.

There are many tools you can use that can help automate your business including programs that manage your customer relationships, handle your email marketing and organize your projects so that you have better time management. There are even programs available that will allow you to have payments automatically deposited so that clients are not required to mail checks for payment.

However, the key to making these automated programs work for you is to design your business to scale. There are a few additional tips to keep in mind that will help you better scale your business even without hiring others or using automation.

Look at your client list. When you began as a freelancer, you probably accepted any work that came your way. The review of your invoices indicated the tasks you were doing that really weren't what you wanted to do. Now it is time to review the client list. Do you have a client who constantly complains about how much your services cost? Do you have the chronic late-payers? How about the client who second-guesses your advice and wants it there way, even though you know their way is wrong?

It is time to remove those clients from your list. As painful as that may be, it is time to focus on clients who value your expertise. A client that pays late, ignores your advice or doesn't see value in your fee is a low quality client. This type of client leads to low quality projects and their referrals to you will more than likely be low quality as well. Contact those clients and let them know that you are streamlining your company and that you will need to refer them to another individual or business who can provide the service for them. Give them several new companies to choose from and then move on with clients whc do appreciate you.

The client may surprise you and request that you keep working with them. If that should happen, clearly outline what you expect from them and what they can expect from you. The best part about retaining a client that you were ready to drop is that you have a 60 to 70 percent chance of selling to an existing client and only a 5 to 20 percent chance of selling to a new prospect. Look at ways you can deliver more value to the customers you currently have as a way to grow your business.

Once you have designed your business to scale, it is time to look at making your work predictable so that you are able to systemize your processes.

Chapter 8 – Standardizing

Something most freelancers do not do that you must do as a business is to standardize your processes so that they can be automated. The biggest key to growing your business is the ability to automate some of the things you do on a regular basis. Think of the tasks you do that have to be done, but that bring in no income. Those are the tasks that you may be able to automate.

The majority of freelancers have the mindset that because their work is unpredictable, there is no way to actually automate what they do. They may be concerned that their work will become more like an assembly line. This is definitely not what the goal is when you standardize your processes.

Take meetings for example. When you are sitting in a meeting, whether with a client, vendor or anyone else, you are not getting any work done. Even if the meeting is productive, chances are you lost a significant amount of time discussing things that had nothing to do with the project. In addition, statistics show that the time directly before and immediately after a meeting are dead time for most people, adding to the time lost doing tasks that must be completed. Before scheduling a meeting, set a time limit for that meeting and do not deviate from that time limit. This forces both you and the other people you are meeting with to stick to the subject matters that must be discussed so that you don't drift off into conversations about Monday Night Football.

Begin by creating a list of all the time you will need to communicate with your client. Be sure to include all types of communication, such as email, phone and Skype as well. Be sure to include several follow-up contacts throughout the list, such as after you have sent the proposal, after you send an invoice and after the project is complete. You don't need to list follow-up during the project as you will more than likely be in contact with the client at that point. However, many freelancers forget follow-up requirements when a proposal or invoice has been sent. You may not need those follow-ups, but it is best to assume that you will.

Once you have determined the communication points with clients, identify what action must be taken at each of those points. For example, the day after sending the proposal, you may email the client thanking them for reviewing it. A week later, you may need to check on the status of the proposal if you have heard nothing.

If you are working with a team, assign responsibility for each of these communication points to someone else on the team. If you are still working alone, create templates for each action in order to streamline and standardize the process. Create a list of the correspondence points, who is responsible for them and the file name of the template, keeping it readily available so that you can automatically deal with the various contacts with the client.

This is just one example of standardizing your process so that they are more easily managed. Instead of handwritten lists of things-to-do, you have a process so that the entire project runs as smoothly as possible. By creating a standardized process, it is much easier to automate this portion of your business using project management software or other electronic methods for making sure all of your "t's" are crossed and your "I's" are dotted.

Once you have determined what processes can be standardized so that you can easily perform them systematically, it is time to begin streamlining your business in order to boost speed, efficiency and value.

Chapter 9 – Streamlining

The next step in moving from freelancer to business owner is to begin streamlining your processes which is one of the most important ways to begin building revenue with fewer hours. As we have discussed before, automating is critical to streamlining the things you do on a daily basis. One tip, however, is to add personal touches to any templates you use so clients do not feel as if they are getting canned responses.

Pay attention to the hours that provide the most **productivity** for you. Some people may work best in the morning hours, but struggle to focus in the afternoon. You may find that you work best overnight when everyone else in your house is asleep. Focus on working those hours and you will find that you tend to work more efficiently.

Streamlining processes should make them more predictable, efficient and effective. When we talk about streamlining, we are not necessarily talking about automating services, as not all services can be automated. Yes, some of the day-to-day tasks, such as invoicing or social media posting can be automated, but you certainly can't automate a blog post or a press release. In fact, it is better to streamline manually at first so that you understand the process before you attempt to use software to do it for you.

The first step in streamlining is to list all of the tasks that must be performed to complete a project. You should then list all the software you will use and the required skills necessary. Do not leave out any steps, even the ones that you feel should be automatic. Once you have completed the list, review to see where you can streamline the process.

Let's look at that blog post example. Your company is responsible for the monthly blog posting for a client as well as social media posts that will link to that blog. The steps you will need to follow include:

1. Consulting with the client about the blog post topic.
2. Identify key phrases that pertain to the blog post.
3. Perform necessary research on the subject.
4. Write the blog.

5. Locate or create a graphic to include in the blog.
6. Upload the blog to the client's site using Wordpress.
7. Post a link to the blog on social media.
8. Write three additional social media posts to promote the blog.
9. Schedule the three additional posts using Buffer.
10. Review performance of the blog and social media posts a few days later.
11. Respond to social media comments related to the blog.
12. Respond to comments on the blog.

Once you have listed all the tasks involved in creating the blog and social media posts, note the software you will need to perform the tasks. From this list, it appears that you will use Wordpress, Buffer and probably word processing software, such as Microsoft Word. You will also use search engine software to do your research.

Next, you want to note the specific skills you will use to complete the project. A skills assessment will be important when you are ready to delegate assignments in the future as you are going to want to hire someone with those particular skills. In addition, when you are working to streamline your processes, identifying particular skills is important to the decisions you make during the process.

In this case, you will draw on your writing and research skills to create the blog as well as graphic arts skills in choosing the proper graphic. You will need basic search engine knowledge as well as an understanding of social media. Your communications skills will be necessary both in interactions with the client and with posters on social media or the blog.

Now, review the entire process to see where things can be streamlined. Do you need to meet with the client about the blog topic? Why not create a simple form that the client can complete each month to send you the topic they want to discuss? The writing portion will need to be done manually, but you can set up a template with all the components laid out in outline form to be sure everything is included. Creating a graphic may be time consuming, so it might be better to gather stock graphics that can be adjusted in Photoshop in order to make it easier each month. Use a matrix service that provides you with statistics for your blog and social media all in one report to make it easier to share with the client.

These are just a few examples of how you can streamline processes to free time in your day and begin focusing your time on tasks that will grow your business.

Chapter 10 – Documenting Workflow

Once you have streamlined your tasks as much as possible, it is time to begin documenting your workflow. The more efficient your workflow is, the more work you can complete. One way to document your workflow is by creating an operations manual for your business. Remember, you are no longer working as a freelancer and every successful business has an operations manual that lays out exactly what employees are expected to do on a daily basis. Your company should have one as well.

Because you have gone through the steps necessary to standardize your work as well as make it more streamlined and efficient, you already have the steps ready to create the operations manual. However, there are a few strategies you should follow when creating the business and operations manual to avoid pitfalls down the road.

An operations manual is a reference that you and other employees can use as a reminder of how your business is designed to flow. The operations manual provides information when you are not available or when change needs to be implemented due to a change in the industry or the focus of the business. It is also a valuable tool when training staff.

An operations manual should be neat, organized and as accurate as possible. In fact, many companies refer to it as a living document as you will need to update it on a regular basis as processes change. In fact, some experts say that an operations manual with no notations, highlights or bent pages is not being used, making it ineffective as a tool in your company.

You need to include everything that is critical about your processes. All standard operating procedures should be included in the manual with the appropriate level of detail. Be sure to explain why the procedures are important and connect different processes together so that the reader understands the need for the steps included.

For example, your operations manual may include the steps for the blog and social media posts, but they may be listed separately. This may be because you perform social media functions for one client, but do not handle their blog posting, while another client may contract your company for both. If you have them listed separately, you will want to add a link between the two so that those who are reading the manual understand why they may need to follow both sets of instructions.

In most cases, you can create your business and operations manual from the information you collected during your streamlining process. Once you have finished streamlining, you should be able to create a simple document that explains the steps, in order, that should be taken to complete specific projects. By placing the details for all processes in one, easy-to-use location, staff is less likely to miss tasks or deadlines as long as they are aware that the manual exists.

Even if you are the only person working in your business right now, creating an operations manual is beneficial because it also keeps you on task while preparing your company for the time when you will be able to bring in more help.

So, what exactly will be included in the operations manual? Your standard operating procedure.

Chapter 11 – Structuring a Procedure

One of the main components of the operations manual will be your standard operating procedure (SOP). This document describes, step-by-step, how you want projects completed. A standard operating procedure insures consistent results and gives you reassurance that your clients will receive what you promised them.

A well-written SOP will include three tiers of information:

1. Overview, purpose and scope
2. Definitions, policies and high-level processes
3. Detailed information, how-to steps, checklists and recording

Let's break these tiers down.

You want to be sure anyone who reads the SOP understands the instructions so that they utilize them correctly. When people are unclear about instructions, things are often left undone. Therefore, in the overview section, you should include requirements related to training and responsibility. You should also include information about governance, records and even history related to why this procedure was established.

The definition tier includes flowcharts for complicated processes, approvals that are required and high-level decision making policies. Remember that as your company grows, you will need to move important decisions to higher employee levels so that the basic decisions are made at the lowest levels. In other words, the blogger you hire to write a company blog will not make the decision regarding the blog topic. Instead, that decision will fall to someone at a higher level.

The second tier should also include any definitions, terms or acronyms that you use in your company. For example, you may need to explain what SEO is in case a new hire is unfamiliar with the term. Policies related to the procedures should also be included in the second tier. Just remember to update the policies in the SOP if they change. This is the area of the SOP where you include what to do if something should go wrong. If Buffer goes down and does not send out your schedule post, what should be done? Although it may seem intuitive that you would simply post manually, it is possible someone who is new or unfamiliar with the process may not know they are permitted to do that. Flowcharts are an excellent addition to this section of the SOP as they allow someone to quickly determine the next steps to take.

The final tier includes the in-depth information and will be the largest section of the document. This is where the step-by-step instructions are found, checklists can be added and how-to steps are provided. Flowcharts are also beneficial in the third tier.

The SOP should be updated on an annual basis to be sure that any minor changes that have been implemented throughout the year are included. All SOPs should be combined into one binder or notebook with a table of contents to make it easier for staff to locate and use the information.

Now that you have put together your standard operating procedures, it is time to talk about hiring people who may need to use those documents.

Chapter 12 – Delegating

So, your processes are standardized and streamlined, your workflow documented, and your SOP ready to go. Now it is time to learn how to delegate responsibilities to other people. For some, removing themselves from their work can be a difficult process. Freelancers are used to doing everything by themselves so it may be difficult to hand the work over to someone else. In addition, it is important to know when it is time to begin hiring for your company.

"How do I know when it is time to hire?" is a common question asked by people who are shifting from freelancer to business owner. There are a few questions whose answers may indicate when it is time to bring other people in to help you in your business:

- Are you spending all your time doing employee work rather than CEO work?
- Could a part-time person, one day per week, relieve your workload?
- Can you afford the total cost of an employee, including salary, benefits, taxes and the responsibility of providing enough work to keep them busy?
- What costs would you incur if you don't hire?

If the answer to the first question is yes, it may be time to look into hiring someone to help. If you hire someone to handle the $15 per hour work, you can focus on the $300 per hour work. You may just start with someone who handles your bookkeeping or who social media postings, but since someone else is doing those tasks, you are freed up to do others.

You may only need to hire someone for a few hours for one day per week. Maybe it is someone to do your housecleaning or a virtual assistant to handle your correspondence. Don't forget that you don't have to bring on a paid employee. You can hire a contractor or work through online sites that provide assistance, such as content writing. By using a contracted employee, you may find that the third question is easily answered "yes" as the costs are significantly lower if you do not have to offer benefits or pay taxes for a full-time employee.

Remember that you are building a business, so it is critical that you look at the long-term needs of your company. Hiring means a long-term commitment to an employee, so make sure your revenue can support the costs of hiring. If you are struggling to meet ends meet for your own household, it is not the time to hire. If the company has grown to the point you are struggling to keep up with demand, a contractor may be the answer.

What will happen if you don't hire? Craig Jennings of Powhatan Consulting says "Running a lean staff is like running an engine with the minimum amount of gas. Sometimes, running in neutral is the right things to do, but you can't manage normal traffic without using gas." In other words, if you are not hiring just because you are being frugal, consider that your competitors may not be protecting their cash quite as closely. It may be time to look into hiring someone to reduce your own workload and allow you to focus on growing the business even more.

So, once you have decided it is time to hire, how do you learn to delegate jobs to someone else when you have been doing them yourself for so long? One way is to prioritize the tasks you do on a daily basis. Assess which tasks you want to continue to perform as well as those you excel at doing. Anything that you don't do well, such as tracking finances or sales, delegate that to someone else. Delegate tasks that you don't enjoy doing as well, as if you don't enjoy doing it, you probably don't do it well.

Some of the most commonly delegated tasks when a freelancer begins moving toward becoming a business owner include:

- Administrative tasks
- Bookkeeping or accounting
- Web development and maintenance
- Writing
- Lawn or house care
- Laundry
- Cooking

Once you have decided to delegate tasks, remember that not everyone works in the same way. Start by delegating small projects or a portion of a large project as a test. Allow extra time in case they do not deliver or provide a written schedule to see if the person can deliver ahead of time. If they deliver good work ahead of a deadline, they are probably a good fit for your organization.

Communication is key in delegation. As a freelancer, you know that there may be ten projects in the works at the same time and you don't want people sitting around waiting for someone to get their portion done so that the next step can begin. By clearly communicating deadlines and checking on the progress periodically, you should be able to trust that those you have delegated jobs to will complete them on time.

One of the most important things about delegating is the need to give feedback on the work that is completed. Unfortunately, many supervisors are quick to point out what is wrong in a project and rarely offer praise for jobs well done. Be sure to comment when a graphic is particularly good or if a blog is absolutely perfect.

Plan for problems by always having a backup plan. Never set a deadline for an employee on the same day you are supposed to deliver it to the client. Always give them a deadline a few days prior in case you have to revise something. Even someone who has done consistent work for you in the past can have a bad day, providing work that is not up to par. By preparing a backup plan, you will still be able to meet the client deadline.

Be sure to share any positive feedback from the client with your team as well. Success is why people work on the team and when a project succeeds it is important to share that success with those who made it happen.

There are even websites designed around delegation. TaskRabbit connects people in communities on the premise of "neighbor helping neighbor," while Fancy Hands is a virtual assistant company. Agent Anything connects people with college students who are able to do small jobs, run errands or accomplish tasks. GigWalk is an on-demand mobile workforce whose members have performed everything from field audits to mystery shopping, while Swappin lets professional service companies swap tasks. These are just a sample of the many different ways you can find people to delegate tasks to without having to hire a full-time employee.

Delegation does not have to be a scary thing, even if you are used to doing everything by yourself. By following a few easy steps, you will find yourself able to focus more on growing your business and less on the mundane, day-to-day tasks that eat up your time.

The question now is how to go about hiring those people who will be doing these tasks for you.

Chapter 13 – The Hiring Process

You have made the decision to hire people to help you in your business. The problem is that you have no idea how to go about hiring the right people to do the tasks you need done. Whether you are hiring contractors, interns or employees, there are some steps you should take to be sure you choose the right person for the job.

The first thing to do is to write a job description. Make a list of all the tasks you have decided to delegate along with some information about the company. If you have decided to hire an employee, post the job description on job boards like Monster or Careerbuilder. You can also post them on niche job boards like Mashable or Cloroflot. You may be surprised to learn that some of the best places to look for new hires is by asking your connections. A friend, family member or colleague may know someone who would be perfect for the position.

Instead of hiring employees, many freelancers who are moving toward becoming business owners contract with other freelancers. Again, your network of friends, family and colleagues may reveal someone who is willing to work for you on a contracted basis. You can also find freelancers on a wide range of websites, many of whom allow you to hire the freelancer through them.

If you do choose to use a freelancer, remember that they are not full-time employees, but that does not mean a good freelancer should be taken advantage of. You were a freelancer once. Treat them as you wanted to be treated by clients. Provide them with clear guidelines and pay them fairly, on time. If you use a website, they may handle the payment to the contractor for you. For example, content writing sites often ask clients to put money in an escrow account so that the writer is paid as soon as the assignment is completed to the satisfaction of the client.

If you have decided to hire a part- or full-time employee, be sure that you have a defined role for the employee, which is why you should create the job description before you begin searching for staff. When it is time for the interview process, follow these tips:

- Past experience – What did they do in the past? Have they ever worked for a startup? Why did they leave?
- Values – The candidates' values should match your own, especially when it comes to work-life balance, long-term goals and attitude.
- Passion – Since you are basically a start-up company, you want someone who has a passion for your specialty. If the candidate gives the impression that they are just going to put in time for your company, they may not be a good fit.
- Don't settle – A bad fit can be devastating to a company, especially one that is just starting out.
- Have an open-mind – Think of hiring like dating – if you aren't open to different possibilities, you may be sitting home on Saturday night.

Finally, once you have chosen the perfect candidate, you need to develop an onboarding process. This is a method to insure that your new hire is productive as quickly as possible. A good onboarding process begins long before the employee starts working. Instead of having the employee fill out tons of paperwork on the first day, consider sending a welcome packet to their home so they can fill it out before they arrive.

The first day the employee begins working, don't throw a ton of information at them. A new hire may be too nervous to ask questions and if you provide them with too much data, they won't remember it. Present only the basics in an easy-to-understand method. Engage the employee in conversation, giving them a chance to give insight into their personal goals. Be sure that the employee understands how they can provide individual contributions to the company. This personal approach will put the employee more at ease and let them see that they have a career path in the company, even if they are currently the only staff member.

Onboarding should continue for several months, not at the end of the employee's first week. There are many experts who believe that an employee should be provided training for the first year as it takes one year to work through all the cycles of a business.

You have now hired your first staff member, whether it is an employee or a freelancer. This means you will be able to delegate tasks and take the first step as a business owner. It is now time to begin marketing your company.

Section 3 – Market

Chapter 14 – Marketing a Product

Now it is time to get out there and sell your productized services to customers. One of the biggest mistakes small businesses make is to think of marketing as advertising. In fact, advertising is only one small part as marketing encompasses many activities designed to promote your company and insure that customers are getting the value they deserve.

The first step in marketing your service as a product is positioning. According to Ann Latham, President of Uncommon Clarity, a marketing company headquartered in Massachusetts, there are six core points that influence a buyer to choose one product over another. They are:

1. A product worth waiting for
2. Pricing
3. Easiest to purchase and use
4. Best customer service and support
5. Exactly what they need
6. Compatibility with customer values

By aligning these influences with your target market, you can better position your marketing strategy. To start, you must identify objectives that meet the needs of your target market. For example, if your niche is blog and social media posts, your target market may find the ease of using your company to take care of this for them is worth any price. Therefore you would move the third item in the list to number one, while you may move the second item in the list to the bottom. We will discuss identifying your customer needs later, but keep this in mind as we talk about how you should position your products in that target market.

So what, exactly, *is* positioning? Positioning outlines what your company should do to market your productized services to potential customers. Positioning creates an image based on the audience through promotion, price, place and product. In fact, positioning your products properly will elevate your marketing plan, making clients more likely to purchase.

Positioning occurs in a variety of areas throughout your marketing process.

Advertisements, location and price all have a place in positioning your services. Advertisements are often the first place where positioning occurs as that is where the customer gets their first glimpse of what your company is about. However, advertising is not the only way that your company will reach out to customers. You must position your product relative to location as well. Finally, much research has been done on price as a marketing strategy. This research indicates that price tells a consumer more about a product than many marketers originally believed. Consumers look at high-priced items as if they are of better quality. If a product is positioned in the middle of the pricing scale for their market, they may position themselves as a better alternative than high-priced brands, while pricing lower in the scale will cause consumers to compare them to lower-priced options.

Positioning is about learning what is unique about your service over the same service offered by another company. However, being different is not the only thing that positions your product. Your product must be attractive to the consumer and be distinctive. It requires strategy to place your brand in the minds of consumers, especially if there are many other companies out there offering the same thing.

In many cases, positioning requires convincing a company that it will benefit them to outsource certain tasks, much like you determined the tasks you could outsource when you learned to delegate. If you are a content writer, it is possible your positioning is more about why the client shouldn't do the work themselves rather than positioning yourself as better than the competition.

There are several different positioning strategies available for service industries. You can position yourself as a service that is different than those offered by competitors, as a low cost option or as a niche market provider. There are also several factors that can guide your positioning, including:

- Attributes – Attribute positioning is based on a single feature of your service. A web designer who has been named as the top designer in a certain area may position themselves as "The Number 1 Web Designer in Happyville, Utah."
- Benefits – If your company offers unique benefits for the client, you would use that attribute to position yourself in the market place. You may be the only web designer with a certain certification, adding to the benefit a client will receive by choosing you over a competitor.
- Use or Application – When your services have been deemed the best, such as winning a prestigious web design award.

- Users – When your product meets the requirements of a specific group or industry, such as a content writer who specializes in legal content.
- Competitor – A product that is positioned against a particular competitor.
- Category – A position that describes your service as a leader in that category. Think of Xerox, a company whose name is synonymous with copiers or Kleenex, a word many people use instead of tissue. This is more like household name positioning.

There are some cautions when positioning your product, however. It is important not to over- or under-position as consumers may fail to notice the brand. Be sure that you communicate features and benefits clearly without redundancy. One of the biggest mistakes companies make when positioning their brand is by making promises that seem impossible to keep. If a consumer perceives that you are unable to do what you say you can do, they will not choose your brand.

Now that you have determined what your position should be in the market, it is time to determine what that market should be. Let's learn the steps for identifying your target market.

Chapter 15 – Know Your Customer

It is now time to understand who you think will purchase your productized service. Having a clear vision of who your target market is increases your chance of success, no matter what type of business you operate. This is especially true of freelancers who want to move into the position of business owners. As a freelancer, you probably accepted work from anyone who would hire you. Now that you are selling a service as a product, you need to identify where the most potential income will come from and how your service will benefit that particular market.

Too often, startup businesses think that a target market will limit their business, but that is not the case. Identifying a target market does not prevent you from accepting clients who are outside the range of that market, but gives your marketing plan a focus so you don't waste resources marketing to clients who will probably never want to use your services.

Your marketing resources are going to be limited, so it is important to make the most of what you have to work with. In your mind, you may look at the website you created as marketing to the entire world, using the "if I build it, they will come" attitude. However, if you are a web designer, only those who are seeking someone to design a website are going to search for your company and even fewer are actually going to click on your website after a Google search to see what you offer. Fewer still will actually become clients.

Focusing on a specific target market reaches out to the people who are more than likely going to use your services, making it even more likely that someone who clicks on your website is going to become a client. The key is to define your target market properly.

In most cases, freelancers work with businesses, not individuals. This means that your business will probably be known as a "business-to-business" or "B2B" company. Therefore, creating a target customer is slightly different than it would be for a company that markets to individuals.

The first step is to develop a set of common characteristics for your typical customer. These characteristics are often a combination of:

- Industry size
- Number of employees
- Amount of annual sales
- Geographic location

One way to begin developing a customer profile is to interview or survey current clients. Ask questions that include:

- How did they find your company? Was it word-of-mouth, online, etc.?
- What was it that made them choose your company? Price? Customer Service? Uniqueness?
- What level of experience do they have? This question will be tailored to your industry. A content writer may ask what writing experience a client may have while a web designer may ask about technical experience.
- Detailed information about the company, such as size, type, industry, etc.
- Location
- What challenges do you face?
- What problem or product does our service solve for you?
- Evaluate our sales process – was it easy, hard, complicated, etc.

For some industries, you may want to include questions on demographics, such as age, gender and income, but not all industries will need that data.

Unlike creating a single-customer persona, a business persona focuses on the priorities of the business, not what that individual position needs. What objectives do the majority of your clients have in their daily workload? What obstacles do the majority of them face?

Let's say you, as a content writer, interview ten clients. Of those ten clients, the objective for six of them is to build a stronger online presence using better content and social media. Two of them need website copy updated and the last two simply need the occasional blog written. None of the ten clients have any writing expertise but four of them have social media experience. From this demographic, you can focus your marketing on companies who need a stronger online presence whose staff has limited writing experience. Although you will still provide services for the clients who need less of your service, your main focus is on clients who need more of your services.

You can also develop what is known as a niche market which is especially helpful for companies whose services are unique. A photographer that specializes in official corporate photos has a niche market. They would market to people who need professional headshots for their employment, such as lawyers or real estate agents. A content writer with a strong legal background may create a niche market specifically geared toward law offices.

Once you have determined what makes up your target market, it is time to begin looking at your marketing plan. The first step is understanding the three-step sales funnel and how three key metrics can simplify your marketing efforts.

Chapter 16 – 3-Step Sales Funnel

If you ask any freelancer what their reasons are for not becoming a business owner, the majority of them will say it is because they don't know how to market their business. Even after identifying their target market, many freelancer's get the deer-in-the-headlight look when you start talking about marketing plans. Therefore, I want to put this in terms that will be very simple to understand and follow so that you are able to easily market your own business to clients.

One of the easiest ways to look at marketing is as if it is a funnel, with the widest part at the top and the narrowest part at the bottom. The funnel consists of the stages a consumer goes through before they make a purchase. On the consumer side of the funnel, there are five stages a customer goes through when making the decision to purchase a product. These include:

- Awareness of a product or service
- Contemplation of the purchase
- Preference for brand, model or competitor
- Making the purchase
- Brand loyalty and advocacy

On the business side, however, there are three stages that a marketing plan should focus on in order to shorten the length of the sales cycle. These stages are:

- Lead Generation
- Lead Nurturing
- Customer Acquisition and Expansion

At the top of the sales funnel is lead generation. This is the widest section of the funnel as all potential clients are in this section. Leads are any potential clients who are either referred to you by others or who you connect with through your own networking efforts. It may be a new client who filled out the "contact us" form on your website or one who saw the work you did for another client. Regardless of how they were generated, it is critical at this stage of the sales funnel to nurture those leads.

Research shows that nurtured leads produce a 20 percent, on average, increase in sales over those that are not nurtured. In addition, organizations that nurture leads experience a 45 percent increase in their return-on-investment.

First, you must create the lead generation part of your sales funnel. You can do this through social media, your website, email blasts or any number of ways. Leads come from a wide range of sources. Other clients may recommend you for services or you may meet someone at a trade show who is looking for someone to perform the tasks you do. No matter how you connect with the potential client, once the lead has been generated, they move into the next section of the funnel, the nurturing section.

So, how do you nurture those leads? Well, if you have been focusing on your target market, the leads generated should be quality leads as they are more likely to move down the funnel to the next stage. Some tips for nurturing those leads:

1. Develop an instant response system in the form of an email that lets the lead know you will be contacting them. The email should include information about where you connected with them and an idea of wher and how you will get in contact. In the email, ask for additional information so you can be better prepared when you do reach out to them. Offer a discount or special offer for quick response from them. Make sure to contact them as you said you would.
2. Offer immediate value, such as a "how-to" guide or other gift. This should be something that benefits the potential client even if they don't become a client.
3. Try to understand what it is the prospect needs and develop methods for meeting that need even before you contact them.
4. Provide the lead with several different contact methods – email, cell phone, social media.
5. Ask how the prospect prefers you contact them in the future. Not only does this let them know you plan to stay in touch, but also allows you to reach them in their preferred method.
6. Keep in touch, but do not be too pushy.
7. Offer additional value, such as an e-book or combine different services to create a package that will benefit the potential client in more than one way.

When the customer makes a purchase or signs a contract, they move into the final section of the sales funnel which many marketers think is the most important. This section involves follow-up so that the customer develops loyalty to your brand. Once a lead becomes a customer, your marketing efforts must shift slightly. You must provide excellent customer service, continuing to provide the client with high-level services just as you do for new customers.

In this section of the sales funnel, you must actively cultivate relationships with your existing customers, treating those who have already signed on the dotted line exactly as you would new customers. Have you ever been frustrated when you see those advertisements that someone who signs up with your cell phone provider today will be offered a significant discount, but there is no discount offered to the loyal customers who have remained with them for years? When you provide extra service to a new customer but ignore your current customers, you are performing just like the cell phone company.

It is also beneficial to try to upsell current customers, getting them to try additional services you may offer. For example, if a customer initially signed on for you to create their monthly blog posts for a year, when the contract is coming up for renewal, suggest that they let you take over their social media posting as well. You can even offer them a slight discount over a new customer to encourage them to choose the more expensive package.

Create a loyalty reward program. There are many third-party programs available that will set-up and operate a loyalty program for your clients. The reward may range from discounted services to gift cards at local businesses, depending on how elaborate you wish to get with the program.

The key to making sure you are performing well throughout the sales funnel is by measuring these key metrics. There are several ways that you can measure how effective your sales funnel is:

- Measure the traffic and engagement from different types of content.
- Measure your call-to-action click through rates.
- Learn which dedicated landing pages get form fills.
- Track email click rates.
- Track email marketing automation performance.

By tracking these metrics, you will be able to see where your sales funnel needs adjustment and what areas are working well.

Now that you understand how the sales funnel works, let's provide you with some short- and long-term strategies to increase traffic.

Chapter 17 – Building Traffic

If you are a web designer or content writer, you already know the importance of traffic in getting business online. I cannot stress enough that the "Field of Dreams" attitude will not work with today's massive internet. Clients are unlikely to simply stumble on your website and think "Wow! That's exactly what I was looking for!" Instead, you need strategies that work like an online GPS that will guide potential clients to your site.

What is interesting is that it is often something small that brings your service to the attention of a potential customer. It may be as small as your website address on your business card or in the signature of an email. Some online discussion groups and chats permit you to add your company website to your profile. Since those discussion groups allow you to demonstrate your expertise or provide solutions, having your URL in your profile may lead a member of the group to click through to your website.

Create a social media page for your business and post there often, adding links to topics relevant to your industry. Did you come across an article on the latest SEO practices? Add a link to your social media site. This is a simple way to keep your social media page up-to-date and to add value for search engines.

Email is still one of the best ways to reach current and potential customers, but be sure to ask clients to opt-in and make it very simple for them to opt-out. Consider creating a monthly newsletter with helpful tips and suggestions related to your industry. Be sure to include fun things in the newsletter as well, such as quirky trivia questions. Add funny cartoons or pictures, such as your dog in reindeer antlers or yourself decked out in green for St. Patrick's Day. Be sure to include hyperlinks so that customers can simply click to be taken to a site with more information.

You want to keep the word "viral" in mind with every email, newsletter and social media post. You want others to share your information, so make it as easy for them to do so as possible. In addition, make sure your blog posts and white papers have headlines that will grab a reader's attention. Think about the magazines by the grocery store checkout. Do you think the *National Enquirer* would sell as many papers with a headline that read "Blake Shelton Seen At Dinner With Cousin" rather than "Blake Shelton Spotted Dining With Young Brunette?" Your headline needs to be just as attention grabbing as those of the supermarket tabloids.

There are hundreds of tips for getting traffic to your website, from using the proper keywords to submitting content to aggregator sites. The fact is that getting your company website address into the hands of your target market is the key to success. The more often you can do that, the better chance that a potential client will search for your company online.

One new concept in driving traffic and gaining customers is through education marketing. This strategy allows you to convert leads to customers by teaching.

Chapter 18 – Education Marketing

One concept in marketing that is gaining ground is converting leads by teaching customers to solve their own problems. Empowering clients creates a stronger loyalty than other forms of marketing, yet very few companies use this approach to converting clients.

Let's use the content writer as an example. Someone has reached out to you about writing press releases for their company. During the initial meeting, the client brings up their website so you can get a feel for their voice. You notice that the copy on the site is outdated and know that you can help this client. Rather than try to sell them the package outright, you could point out the copy that seems outdated and suggest that they talk to their web design firm about correcting the problem. Provide them with samples of copy just as a suggestion. You have just provided the client with a solution to a problem, creating the belief in their mind that you are an expert at what you do. The client may want to contract with you to rewrite copy on the website, or they may choose to do it themselves, but it will remain in their minds that you offered them a solution.

When you teach someone, you create value. Although you may have already noticed the website copy before your meeting, waiting until the client showed you the site made it seem as if you just happened to notice the problem. The client may feel as if you have just offered them something of value without asking for anything in return.

You provide a teaching experience when you share an interesting article, written by someone else, on your social media pages. Content that teaches contains value, so even if it is not something you have written, you have given potential clients the impression that you want to help them learn about your business.

If you ask any teacher why they went into the teaching profession, they will tell you it was to inspire their students to achieve great things. That is exactly what you are doing when you use teaching as a marketing tool.

There are other ways that you can use teaching in your marketing mix. White papers, blogs and other online informational documents are an excellent way to provide information to current and potential clients. A blog post on new Google algorithms provides customers with insight into the complex world of search engines. Although the client may understand it after your explanation, your call-to-action letting them know that they can learn more if they contact you indicates that you can help them understand it even more. Better still, they may decide they don't want to understand it and reach out to you for help.

Never discount the importance of teaching a client to solve their own problem rather than solving it for them. You will not only create the view in their minds that you are an expert in the field, but could also achieve stronger loyalty from them due to the trust you build.

Chapter 19 – Your Sales Page

So, we have learned how to productize our services, delegate tasks, identify our target market and create a marketing plan. It is time to put it all together and create a sales page that works. There are several tips and strategies that will help you design a sales page that turns leads into conversions.

Be sure to write an interesting narrative. The narrative may tell the story about who they are while others weave a tale that draws in the reader and convinces them that they should purchase products there and only there. One way to do that is by looking at what past clients have said about your work, look at the comments on your blogs or read posts on your Facebook page. Incorporate all of that into the narrative on your sales page.

A good narrative should walk clients through your process so they can see if you will be a good fit for them and them for you.

Your services page should focus on the one thing you do well for customers, which goes back to where you focused your services while you were productizing. Too often, businesses give customers too many choices and this often leads them to choose none of them.

Provide some education. Remember when we discussed teaching as a marketing technique? This is one of those areas where you can apply that knowledge. A web designer could offer anyone who visits their sales page a free e-course entitled "Common Web Design Mistakes." This course could include one, two or even three common mistakes companies make in their website design. Some of those who get the e-course will simply fix those mistakes and move on, but most will understand that there must be much more you know about web design and approach you for a quote.

Always include how the features of your service benefit the client. Instead of "We provide informative blog posts" say "We provide informative blog posts so that your staff can focus on the important tasks." This builds trust with clients and lets them know what you can do for them.

Include testimonials so that potential clients see that your services are valuable. Often, people trust a company more if others indicate that the company is successful, trustworthy and delivers what they promise. Include statistics whenever possible, such as "Joe's Plumbing increased their website traffic by 52 percent after using our service."

Make it easy for people to reach you as well. One of the biggest complaints people have is that it is difficult to find contact information on websites. Even worse, when a client completes a form on a website and never gets a response from the company. Always have someone check the email account connected with the website on a daily basis and respond to those emails quickly.

Of course, there are nuts-and-bolts items to include on your sales page as well, such as a catchy headline, an easy-to-find purchase button, easy-to-read font and images that are relevant to your company.

It is time, now, to put it all together in a systemized marketing plan.

Chapter 20 – Systemized Marketing

A systemized marketing strategy links the overall marketing strategy to lead generation, follow-up, monitoring and improvement. It lets the overall strategic view of an organization determine how the marketing system is managed.

Let's face it. You didn't go into freelancing or decide to become a business owner so you could spend your entire day marketing. But if you don't market your business, you probably won't succeed. That is why systemized marketing is an excellent option for promoting your company.

The key is to put one marketing system in place at a time. Once that system is operating smoothly, add another and continue until the entire process is automated. You do not have to use every marketing method available. In fact, you should pick a strategic few that will get you in front of clients quickly. Trying to use too many marketing strategies is less effective than choosing a few as you are not able to focus on them all.

This does not mean you will not ever have to market your company again, as that is never going to happen. Instead, schedule a time each week to work on marketing, but when that time is up, move on to the next project. There is also nothing wrong with assigning marketing tasks to someone else, whether you hire an intern, a virtual assistant or assign it to an employee you have recently hired.

So, how do you put your marketing on autopilot? The first step is replicating what you have already done. Use your website to answer commonly emailed questions. A blog post can become press releases and social media posts. Expand a set of blog posts into an e-book. This lets you do more marketing with less effort.

Today, automation can take care of a lot of the marketing for you. If your website is designed properly, it can handle most of your sales and combining it with things like email marketing, microblogging and widgets can automate almost all of your online marketing.

This cannot be said enough, especially to former freelancers who are used to doing everything themselves. Delegate, delegate, delegate. Outsource as much marketing work as you can by using virtual assistants or contractors who have experience in marketing a company that offers your services.

There are also many programs available that can help you automate your marketing efforts so that you are not faced with promoting your company all day, every day. As long as you have productized your services, begun taking steps to hire some help and developed a good target market, your marketing plan may almost run itself.

Conclusion

You now should have a clear understanding of how to move from freelancer to business owner. The steps outlined here will give you a guide to follow so that your company can grow and thrive. You will no longer be a slave to the keyboard, staring out the window as your life passes you by. You can take a vacation. You can enjoy a day off. All it takes is a little work and dedication.

You may be asking yourself how you can apply this information to what you do. You may not understand how you can productize your services and begin applying these concepts to your freelance business. Let's take a quick look at some common freelance positions and see how this could work:

Writers

- Turn a set of blog posts into an e-book for yourself or a client.
- Create ready-made sales letter templates so clients only have to fill in the blanks.
- Create website copy for new or already online websites
- Write regular blog and connection social media posts for companies.
- Develop Standard Operating Procedure or Operations Manuals for companies
- Create Human Resource Manuals.

Designers

- Sell web elements to companies
- Create graphic artwork
- Create icons and imojis
- Develop vector artwork
- Design social media pages
- Create design concepts for marketing plans

Developers

- Create and sell web frameworks with frontend connections to database, basic CSS3 and HTML 5 templates
- Create working ecommerce templates
- Develop unique customer interfaces and dashboards

In all honesty, the possibilities are endless for almost anyone who has worked as a freelancer. The key is to develop a productized service that you can sell without you even working on the project. Put your imagination to work and let's get you going as a business owner.

Kristen Brady is currently a freelance Social Media Consultant and Marketing Writer and one of the leading experts on social media and digital marketing. She is author of How to Use Pinterest, which is published on Amazon. Eric T. Tung named Kristen's business K Brady Service as one of the Top 100 Social Media Power Influencers Houston 2014.

Through her marketing and writing business, Kristen helps businesses of all sizes to accelerate their profits by integrating proven social media and digital marketing strategies. She also travels the Houston and Katy area to share her wisdom and provide social media keynotes and in-depth training. Additionally, Kristen mentors business owners to reach greater heights in their business.

With her popular blog and her large, loyal following on Facebook, Twitter, Google+, Pinterest and LinkedIn, Kristen is considered one of the top resources in the world of marketing.